Music Theory Sample Paper 2020 Grade 3 A
Model Answers

1 Rhythm

1.1 (a) $\frac{4}{4}$ (3)

(b) $\frac{12}{8}$

(c) $\frac{4}{2}$

1.2 (5)

1.3 16 (1)

1.4 compound quadruple (1)

1.5 (1)

(3)

1.7

(1)

2 Pitch

/15

2.1 (a) G♯ (b) A (c) B (6)

(d) E♭ (e) F (f) D♯

2.2 (a) **FALSE** (3)

(b) **FALSE**

(c) **TRUE**

2.3 (a) 𝄞 (b) 𝄢 (c) 𝄢 (d) 𝄞 (4)

2.4 (a) (1)

(b) (1)

3 Keys and Scales

3.1 (1)

3.2 (1)

3.3 (3)

☐   ☐   ✗   ✗   ✗   ☐   ☐

3.4 (a) F♯ minor (3)

   (b) E major

   (c) A minor

3.5 (2)

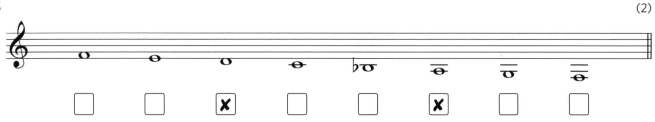

☐   ☐   ✗   ☐   ☐   ✗   ☐   ☐

3.6 X C♯ (2)

   Y G♯

3.7 (a) (1)

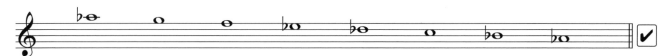   ✔

   ☐

   ☐

(b) (1)

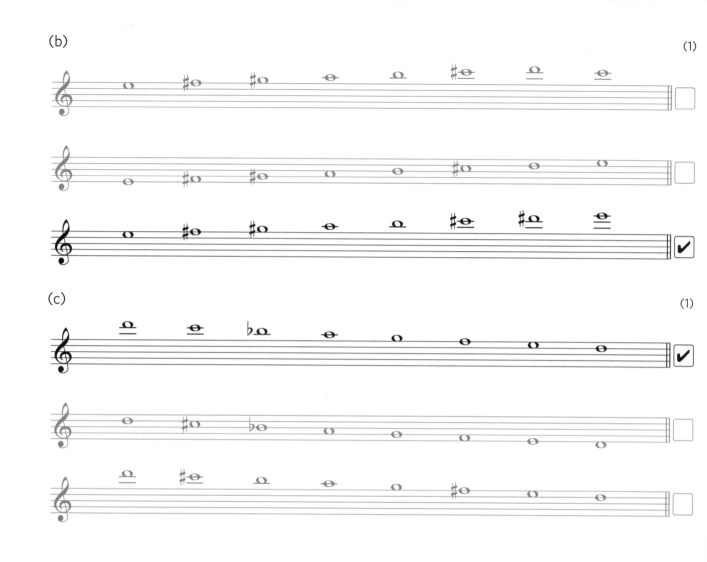

(c) (1)

4 Intervals /10

4.1 (6)

(a)

(b)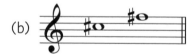

(c)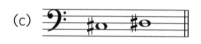

(d)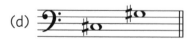

(e)

(f)

4.2 (a) minor (4)

(b) major

(c) perfect

(d) minor

5 Tonic Triads   /10

5.1 (a) **TRUE**   (2)

   (b) **TRUE**

5.2   (3)

(a)    (b)   (c)

5.3 (a) E minor   (5)

   (b) G minor

   (c) D major

   (d) A♭ major

   (e) E major

6 Terms and Signs   /5

semplice means:	**scherzando** means:	*pesante* means:	(5)
simple, plain	playful, joking	heavy	

♩ = 84 means:	*da capo* means:	
84 crotchet beats in a minute	repeat from the beginning	

7 Music in Context   /5

7.1 They are all different from the original   (1)

7.2 TRUE   (1)

7.3 (a) bar 6   (3)

   (b) bar 6

   (c) bar 8

Music Theory Sample Paper 2020 Grade 3 B
Model Answers

1 Rhythm

/15

1.1 (a) $\frac{4}{2}$

(3)

(b) $\frac{6}{8}$

(c) $\frac{3}{8}$

1.2

(5)

1.3 3

(1)

1.4 compound triple

(1)

1.5

(1)

8

1.6   (3)

   ✗   ✗   ✔

1.7   (1)

        ☐   ☐   ✔

2 Pitch   /15

2.1 (a) A♭   (b) B   (c) C♯   (6)

      (d) A   (e) B   (f) D♭

2.2 (a) **TRUE**   (3)

      (b) **FALSE**

      (c) **TRUE**

2.3 (a) 𝄞   (b) 𝄢   (c) 𝄢   (d) 𝄞   (4)

2.4 (a)   (1)

        ☐   ☐   ✔

      (b)   (1)

        ☐   ✔   ☐

3 Keys and Scales

3.1

(1)

3.2

(1)

3.3

(3)

3.4 (a) D minor

(b) E♭ major

(c) F minor

(3)

3.5

(2)

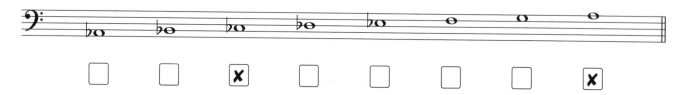

3.6 X E

(2)

    Y A

3.7 (a)

(1)

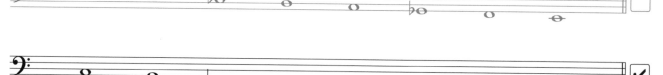

(b)　　　　　　　　　　　　　　　　　　　　　　　　　　　　　　(1)

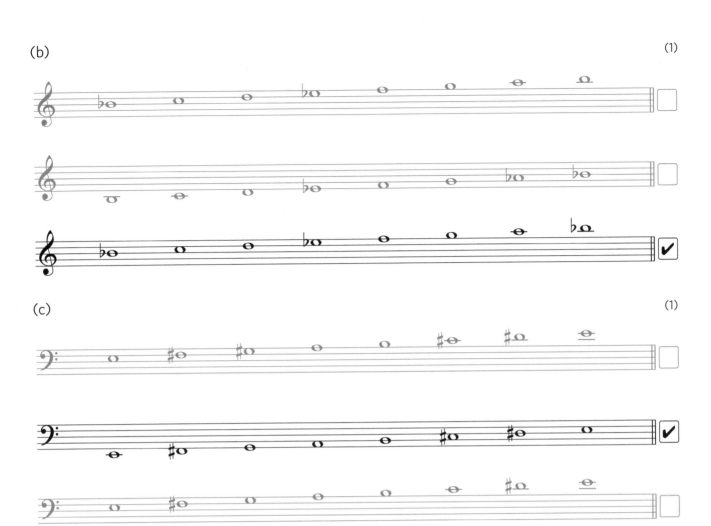

4 Intervals　　　　　　　　　　　　　　　　　　　　　　　　/10

4.1　　　　　　　　　　　　　　　　　　　　　　　　　　　　(6)

 (a)

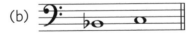 (b)

 (c)

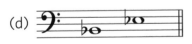 (d)

 (e)

 (f)

4.2 (a) minor　　　　　　　　　　　　　　　　　　　　　　　(4)

　　　(b) minor

　　　(c) perfect

　　　(d) major

5 Tonic Triads

5.1 (a) **FALSE**

    (b) **TRUE**

(2)

5.2

(3)

(a)    (b)    (c)

5.3 (a) F♯ minor

    (b) A major

    (c) A♭ major

    (d) F minor

    (e) B minor

(5)

6 Terms and Signs

/5

maestoso means:

majestic

marcato means:

emphatic, accented

leggiero means:

light

(5)

2 ⊏═══⊐ means:

rest for 2 bars

ritenuto means:

held back

7 Music in Context

/5

7.1 C is an exact copy

(1)

7.2 TRUE

(1)

7.3 (a) D♭

    (b) bar 8

    (c) bar 3

(3)

Music Theory Sample Paper 2020 Grade 3 C
Model Answers

1 Rhythm
/15

1.1 (a) **12/8** (3)

(b) **3/4**

(c) **2/2**

1.2 (5)

(a)

(b)

(c)

(d)

(e)

1.3 4 (1)

1.4 compound duple (1)

1.5 (1)

13

1.6 (3)

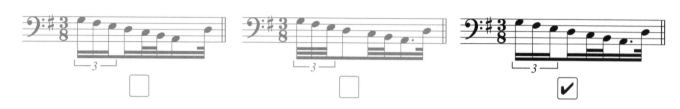

1.7 (1)

2 Pitch   /15

2.1 (a) E   (b) B   (c) A♭   (6)

(d) F♯   (e) F   (f) C♯

2.2 (a) **FALSE**   (3)

(b) **TRUE**

(c) **FALSE**

2.3 (a)   (b)   (c)   (d)   (4)

2.4 (a)   (1)

(b)   (1)

3 Keys and Scales

3.1 (1)

3.2 (1)

3.3 (3)

3.4 (a) G major (3)

(b) F♯ minor

(c) A minor

3.5 (2)

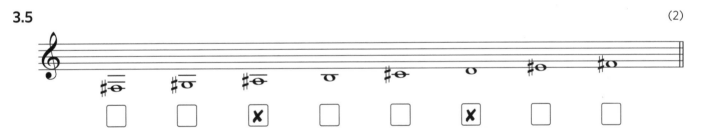

3.6 X D♭ (2)

Y B♭

3.7 (a) (1)

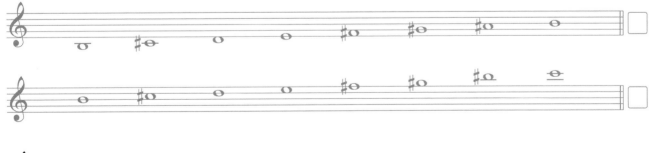

(b)   (1)

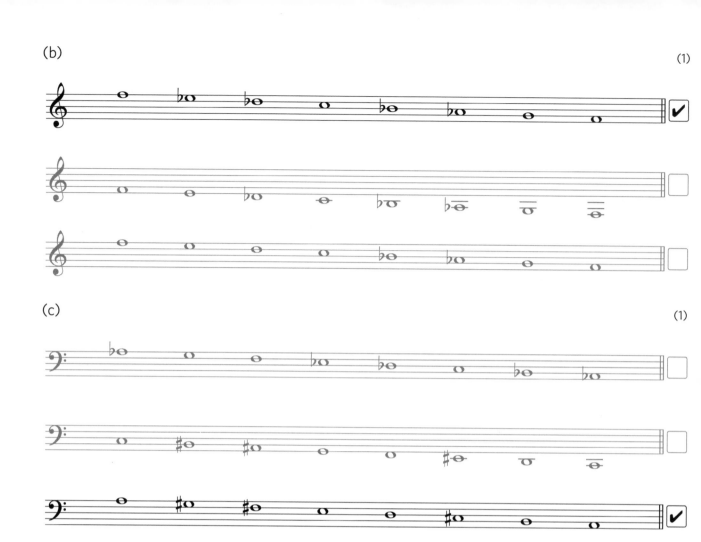

(c)   (1)

4 Intervals   /10

4.1   (6)

(a)

(b)

(c)

(d)

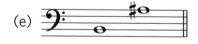
(e)

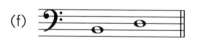
(f)

4.2 (a) perfect   (4)

(b) major

(c) minor

(d) perfect

5 Tonic Triads

5.1 (a) **FALSE** (2)

(b) **TRUE**

5.2 (3)

(a)  (b) (c)

5.3 (a) C♯ minor (5)

(b) F♯ minor

(c) C minor

(d) A♭ major

(e) G minor

6 Terms and Signs

simile means: *triste* means: means: (5)

in the same way   sad, sorrowful   slightly separated

sforzando means: *dolce* means:

forced, accented   sweet

7 Music in Context

7.1 B is an exact copy (1)

7.2 TRUE (1)

7.3 (a) C (3)

(b) bar 5

(c) bar 1

Music Theory Sample Paper 2020 Grade 3 D
Model Answers

1 Rhythm

1.1 (a) $\mathbf{C}$

(3)

(b) $\dfrac{3}{2}$

(c) $\dfrac{9}{8}$

1.2

(5)

1.3 6

(1)

1.4 simple quadruple

(1)

1.5

(1)

1.6 (3)

❌   ✔   ✔

1.7 (1)

☐   ✔   ☐

2 Pitch   /15

2.1 (a) B♭   (b) A♯   (c) E   (6)

(d) F   (e) D   (f) A♭

2.2 (a) **TRUE**   (3)

(b) **FALSE**

(c) **TRUE**

2.3 (a) 𝄞   (b) 𝄞   (c) 𝄞   (d) 𝄢   (4)

2.4 (a) (1)

✔   ☐   ☐

(b) (1)

☐   ☐   ✔

3 Keys and Scales

3.1 (1)

3.2 (1)

3.3 (3)

3.4 (a) G minor (3)

(b) C minor

(c) A♭ major

3.5 (2)

3.6 X G♯ (2)

Y D♯

3.7 (a) (1)

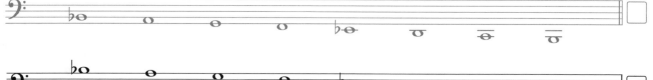

(b)   (1)

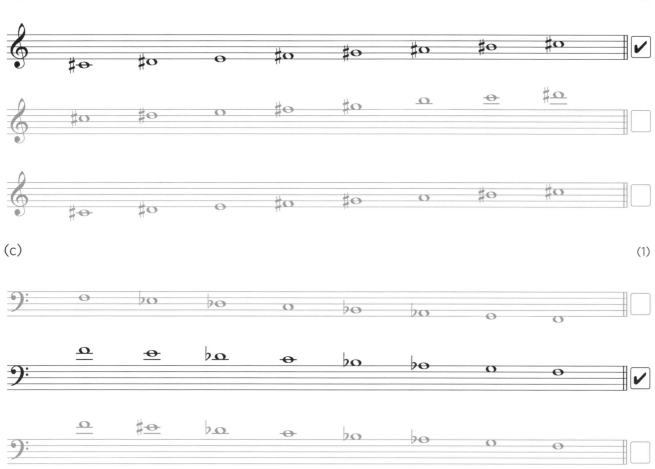

(c)   (1)

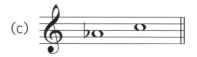

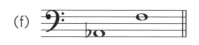

4 Intervals   /10

4.1   (6)

4.2 (a) minor   (4)

     (b) perfect

     (c) minor

     (d) major

5 Tonic Triads /10

5.1 (a) **TRUE** (2)

(b) **FALSE**

5.2 (3)

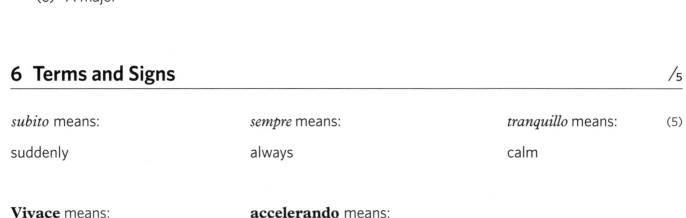

(a)   (b)   (c)

5.3 (a) E minor (5)

(b) F minor

(c) B♭ major

(d) D major

(e) A major

6 Terms and Signs /5

subito means: *sempre* means: *tranquillo* means: (5)

suddenly   always   calm

Vivace means: **accelerando** means:

lively, quick   gradually getting quicker

7 Music in Context /5

7.1 B is an exact copy (1)

7.2 TRUE (1)

7.3 (a) A (3)

(b) bar 6

(c) bar 4